Snap Collective
Publishing

Here
And
There

Julia Laird

Julia Laird is a Scottish photographer based in London. Most of the photographs in this book were taken over the last 10 years on travels and also closer to home. They are all from various cameras and some of the distortions or mistakes are kept in the book as they add to the feeling of the work.

Julia's pictures are like a journey through the kaleidoscope of life - as if by chance she seems to roam around and capture the special with her camera: Beautiful, banal, sad, touching, destroyed. One can hardly look at her photographs without stories playing out before our inner eyes. They are not shots of moments and situations, but blinks from a longer, touching narrative. A narrative of a life lived to the fullest moments.

Dorothee Achenbach, Art historian

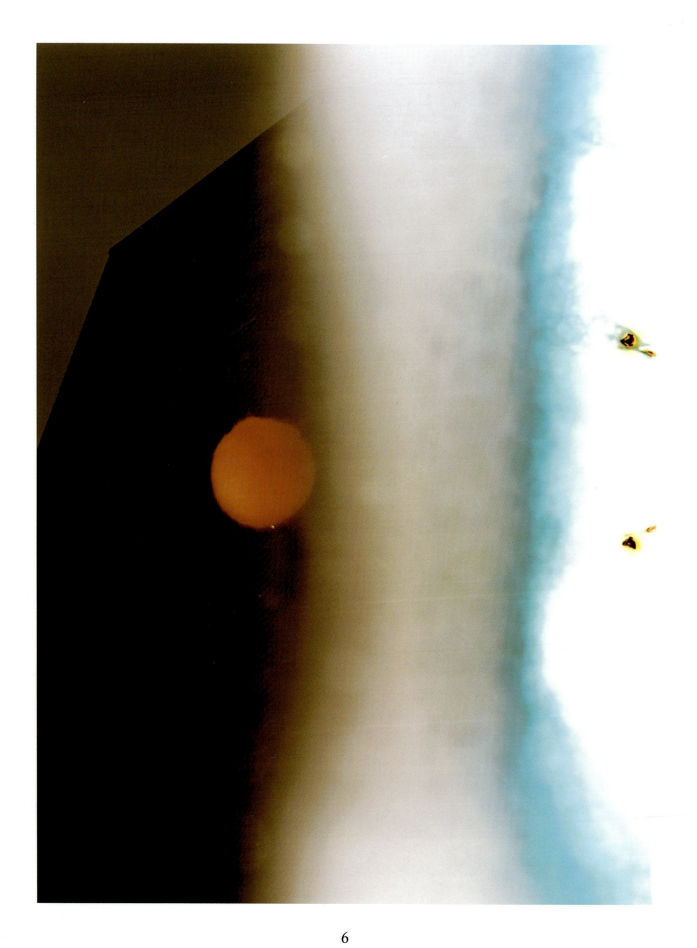

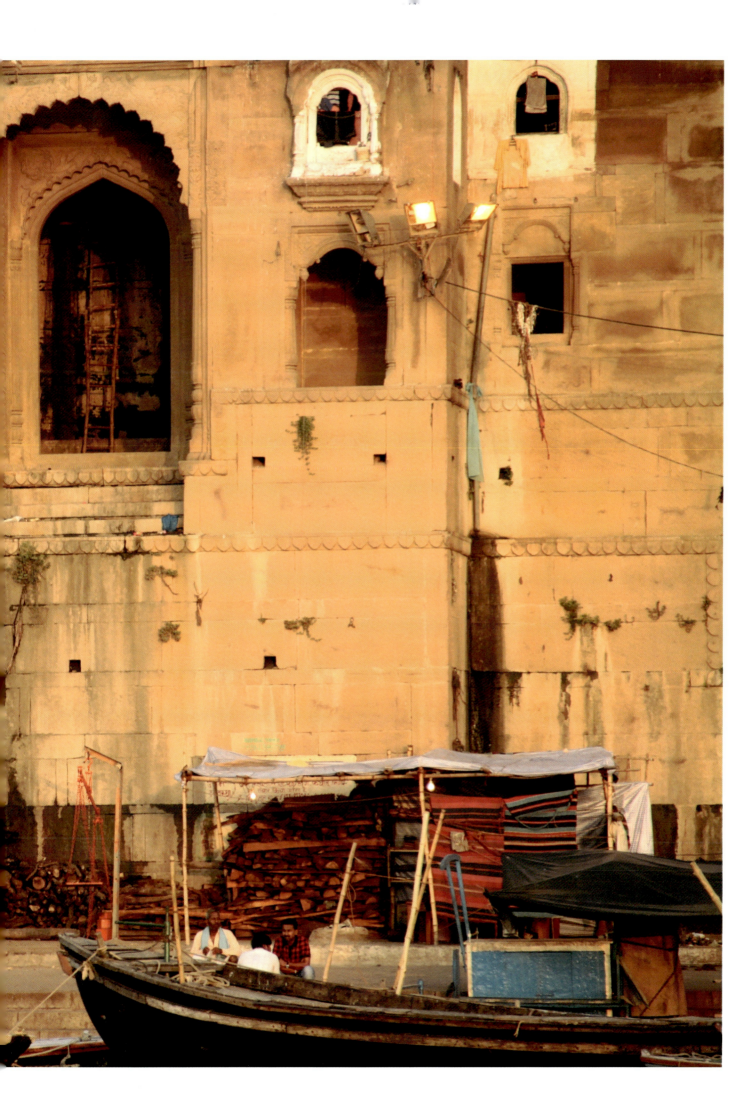

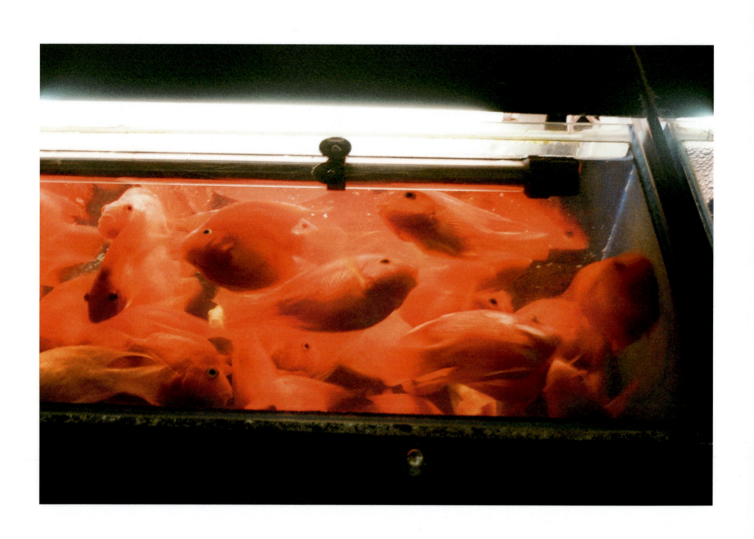

4 - Cornwall, England; Hong Kong.
5 - Hong Kong.
6 - Glasgow, Scotland.
7 - Hong Kong.
8 - Isle of Harris, Scotland;
    Inverewe Gardens, Scotland.
9 - The Highlands, Scotland.
10 - Naples, Italy.
11 - Margate, England; Hong Kong.
12 - Calcutta, India.
13 - Sheffield, England.
14 - London, England.
15 - Kathmandu, Nepal.
16 - Margate, England.
17 - London, England; Hong Kong.
18 and 19 - Hong Kong.
20 and 21 - Hong Kong.
22 - London, England.
23 - Delhi, India.
24 - Hong Kong.
25 - Margate, England.
26 - Monti Della Luna, Italy.
27 - Hong Kong.
28 - Bangalore, India;
    Monti Della Luna, Italy.
29 - Naples, Italy; Dzongri, India.
30 - Naples, Italy.
31 - Varanasi, India.
32 - Puglia, Italy.
33 - Monti Della Luna, Italy.
34 - Naples, India.
35 - Rohtang Pass, India;
    Margate, England.
36 - Yakushima Island, Japan;
    Loch Lomond, Scotland.
37 - Naples, Italy; Amritsar, India.
38 - Glasgow, Scotland.
39 - Annapurna, Nepal.
40 - Hong Kong.
41 - Bikaner, India.
42 and 43 - Hong Kong.
44 - Hong kong; Hong Kong.
45 - Gairloch, Scotland.
46 and 47 - Mathura, India.
48 - Ullapool, Scotland; Hong kong.
49 - Hong Kong.
50 - Hong Kong; Nagano, Japan.
51 - Hong Kong.
52 - Glasgow, Scotland.
53 - Kanyakumari, India.
54 - London, England.
55 - Hong Kong.
56 - North Minch, Scotland.
57 - Delhi, India.

58 - Tokyo, Japan
59 - Osaka, Japan.
60 - Osaka, Japan.
61 - Tokyo, Japan.
62 - Osaka, Japan.
63 - Nagaland, India.
64 - Essaouira, Morocco.
65 - Essaouira, Morocco.
66 - Varimpre, France.
67 - Marrakesh, Morocco.
68 - Sikkim, India.
69 - Varimpre, France.
70 and 71 - Varanasi, India.
72 - Dzongri, India.
73 - Bangalore, India.
74 and 75 - Mathura, India.
76 - Varanasi, india.
77 - Kanyakumari, India.
78 - Nagaland, India.
79 - London, England.
80 and 81 - Varanasi, India.
82 - Delhi, India.
83 - Yakushima Island, Japan.
84 - London, England.
85 - Chennai, India.
86 and 87 - Delhi, India.
88 - Varanasi, India;
    Istanbul, Turkey.
89 - Bucharest, Romania.
90 - Varimpre, France.
91 - Kathmandu, Nepal
    Niort, France.
92 and 93 - Hong Kong.
94 and 95 - Delhi, India.
96 - Hyderabad, India.
97 - Yakushima Island, Japan;
    Bangalore, India.
98 - Alappuzha, India.
99 - Jerusalem, Israel.
100 - Prince Islands, Turkey.
101 - Hampi, India.
102 and 103 - Prince Islands, Turkey.
104 - Bombay, India.
105 - Kushalnagar, India;
    Cornwall, England.
106 - Dzongri, India.
107 - Tokyo, Japan.
108 and 109 - London, England.
110 - Yakushima Island, Japan.
111 - Yakushima Island, Japan.
112 - Bombay, India.
113 - Bombay, India.
114 - Atlas Mountains, Morocco.
115 - Monti Della Luna, Italy.

116 -119 - Hong Kong.
120 - Varimpre, France;
    Nagano, Japan.
121 - Kyoto, Japan;
    London, England.
122 - 125 - Hong Kong.
126 - The Himalayas, India.
127 - Varanasi, India.
128 - Crete, Greece.
129 - Tokyo, Japan.
130 - Tokyo, Japan;
    Hong Kong.
131 - Glasgow, Scotland.
132 - Ladakh, India;
    Hong Kong.
133 - London, England;
    Margate, England.
134 and 135 - Hong Kong
136 - Cornwall, England;
    Puglia, Italy.
137 - Yakushima Island, Japan;
    Puglia, Italy.

Imprint
Any brand names and product names mentioned in this book are subject to trademark, brand or patent protection and are trademarks or registered trademarks of their respective holders. The use of brand names, product names, common names, trade names, product descriptions etc. even without a particular marking in this work is no way to be construed to mean that such names may be regarded as unrestricted in respect of trademark and brand protection legislation and could thus be used by anyone.

Publisher:
Snap Collective
Is a trademark of
Rock N Books Ltd.
59 St. Martin's Lane, Suite 8, London, WC2N 4JS, UK

Printed at: EsserDruck Solutions GmbH Untere Sonnenstraße 5, 84030 Ergolding

ISBN: 978-1-914569-48-7

Design by Alice Shaposhnikova
Editor Maria Lozinska
Copyright: © Julia Laird
Copyright © 2022 Rock N Books Ltd.